TOP TEN½
reasons to read this book

10½. Because it was written by the Mayans one thousand years ago on a prehistoric etch-a-sketch found forty feet below F.A.O. Schwarz.

10. So Dan Quayle won't become President of CBS.

9. Because it makes stupid pet tricks seem more intelligent.

8. So Dave won't go Hollywood and play Moses in the upcoming remake of *The Ten Commandments*.

7. Because it helps prevent the Home Office from being moved to Jurassic Park.

6. Because it is a nonsurgical procedure for adjusting your funny bone.

5. Because it was a smash hit in the future.

4. Because it will definitely inhibit your significant other from channeling Chef Boy-Ar-Dee, Uncle Ben, and H & R Block.

3. Because it operates without batteries and is fully charged.

2. Because it will improve your immune, commune, and buffoon systems.

1. Because you deserve to know everything.

D0521613

THE LUNATIC GUIDE TO

The David Letterman Show*

Bradford Keeney

**A Performance of the Omsemble Orchestra
with Charles Stein, Susan Quasha & George Quasha**

FEATURE CARTOONS BY MIKE THOMPSON
OTHER DRAWINGS BY CHARLES STEIN

Station Hill Press

* There never was and probably never will be a TV show called "The David Letterman Show." (We may be dweebs, but we ain't stupid.)

Published by Station Hill Press, Barrytown, New York 12507.

Cover and book design by Susan Quasha, with assistance from Vicki Hickman.

Text design by Vicki Hickman, Susan Quasha, and Charles Stein.

Drawings on the following pages © 1994 Mike Thompson: Cover, 3, 16, 44, 80, 98, 124, 126.

Drawings on the following pages © 1994 Charles Stein: 9, 12, 15, 17, 18, 21, 23, 24, 25, 26, 33, 35, 37, 38, 46, 49, 51, 52, 53, 54, 55, 56, 57, 61, 62, 63, 64, 65, 66, 68, 70, 72, 77, 82, 86, 88, 89, 93, 101, 102, 103, 105, 107, 108, 111, 115, 116, 117, 125, 127, 128, 129, 130, 143.

The photograph on the frontispiece provided by Reuters/Bettmann.

The following photographs are © 1994 Ripley Entertainment Inc.: *The Giant Electric Light Bulb*, page 42; *The Enormous Broom*, page 123; *The Four Women on the Giant Piano*, page 139.

Library of Congress Cataloging-in-Publication Data

Keeney, Bradford P.
    The lunatic guide to the David Letterman show / Bradford Keeney.
        p.   cm.
    ISBN 0-88268-185-0 : $9.95
    1. Late show with David Letterman. 2. Letterman, David—Humor.
I. Title.
PN1992.77.L39K44   1994
791.45'72—dc20   94-23675
                                                     CIP

"In the beginning was Dave."

(Biblical misprint)

CONTENTS

Around the World With Dave 81

Two Heads Are Crazier Than One 99

The Hidden Meanings of the David Letterman Show 125

Acknowledgements

Standing ovations and multi-cannon salutes to the sources of merriment in my own home — my wife, Marian and my son, Scott, for the many ways they bring joy into my life.

No words can express my glee and ecstasy over the absolutely wild and perfect illustrations contributed throughout this book by the poet and improvisationalist, Charles Stein.

I am also tickled and grateful for the silly madness given to this book by award-winning cartoonist Mike Thompson.*

Deepest bows of appreciation and Olympian leaps of delight to the crazy wisdom shepherds of Station Hill Press — George and Susan Quasha and to Vicki Hickman for successfully juggling hardware, software, and lightning.

And finally, it must be stated that this book would not have been possible it if were not for that former weather man in Indianapolis who once reported that the city was being pelted with hail "the size of canned hams." Thanks, Dave!

*Appreciation also must be expressed for the tickles contributed by Jason Sukut and the *Hessians*, the Letter Men at *The Sports Collection*, Edward Meyer and the amazing wizards of *Ripley's Believe It or Not!*, and especially my first teachers of rascality, W.P. & W.L. Keeney.

Welcome

The Lunatic Guide to The David Letterman Show is an entertainment tool kit filled with stories, cartoons, photographs, and *luna-cises* — wacky, weird and excruciatingly **FUN things to do while watching *Late Show with David Letterman*.** These can be performed for your amusement and enlightenment or just read for the heck of it. If you choose to DO these *lunatic exercises*, we guarantee that you will be in for many other completely indescribable surprises.

There is no better way to get going than to jump head first into this ocean of astonishment and absurdity, so what are you waiting for?

 **On your MARK . . .**
Get SET . . .

(Now you're heading straight for a story that will plunge you right into the silly belly of the *Guide Itself*)

Once upon a time, Ed Sullivan visited Egypt where he presented a command performance of his variety show for the country's royalty. As an expression of their appreciation, a very special tour of the Great Pyramid was arranged. Mr. Sullivan was shown something no other Westerner had ever seen.

A guide took him to a secret chamber unknown to even the greatest archaeologists of the time. Located one kilometer underneath the center of the pyramid's base, the destination took hours to reach by a mechanically driven elevator.

What Ed Sullivan was shown in this secret chamber was a statue of a laughing bull made of gold with an emerald hawk sitting on top of its horns. He was told that he could make one wish while touching the hawk's eye with his left hand and stroking the bull's tail with his right hand. After listening to the guide's instructions he saw the bull and hawk come to life. The bull's lips moved and a sound came out of the hawk's beak saying these words:

The ancient ones taught us that truth is never serious. It can only be given with a twist of humor. If you ask us for anything, we will give it to you as a truth. But as a truth, it will be twisted and turned with divine amusement. You may now put forth your wish.

Ed Sullivan knew what he wanted. He had always desired to have wisdom. As a man in show business, he regretted never having the time to learn the great ideas of the ancient sages. Within seconds, Mr. Sullivan asked the golden bull and emerald hawk for wisdom.

The secret chamber immediately began to shake as if an earthquake were taking place, causing the floor to open.

All that can be said is that Ed Sullivan fell into a tunnel of light that carried him into another time and place. When he finally felt his feet on solid ground, he gathered his wits and looked up to see a great temple with an old sage standing in front of it. The man came up and handed him a business card that had these words of identification:

Socra-tease, WISE GUY

"I'm Socra-tease, guardian of the Three Pillars of Understanding." He went on to give Mr. Sullivan all the wisdom he had ever dreamed of knowing. In the final moment of this transmission of knowledge, Socra-tease left him with this prophecy: "In the future, when you have joined me in the other world, you will be called upon to share this wisdom with readers of a book of truth entitled, *The Lunatic Guide to The David Letterman Show*. The words I have given to you will then help many more generations of television audiences be able to see the really big show. This is our gift to you."

Ed Sullivan never told anyone about his secret tour of that Great Pyramid. Years after he died, his theatre closed. Mr. Sullivan became bored in television heaven and wanted his theatre opened so it would bring some life to those who were watching from above. He asked God if he could return to liven up the dead theatre.

After long consideration, God replied, "You may return to open a show on one condition. It will be necessary for you to share the knowledge given to you by Socra-tease so that new audiences will be able to learn to see the really big show."

Ed Sullivan agreed and within minutes the spirit world chose a man to carry out this mission. This chosen one, known as David Letterman, was mysteriously whisked away* from one television network so he would be able to find his way to The Ed Sullivan Theatre.

Sullivan's theatre once again was given life and Mr. Sullivan, a man of his word, did ask permission to print the wisdom he was given about the three pillars of understanding. These words of truthful wisdom are now delivered to you as understandings necessary to make *The Late Show With David Letterman* become a really big show. Know that these words are all you need to know to fully appreciate the importance of the book you are now reading.

*No TV network could have been dumb enough to let go of David Letterman, so there **must** have been supernatural intervention.

Required for the most powerful reading of this book:

THE THREE PILLARS OF UNDER- STANDING

FIRST PILLAR: **The royal road to self-transformation does not follow the guide-posts of common sense.** It is marked by irrational surprises, uncommon road signs, ridiculous roadside stops, and potholes of absurdity. No other tool of lunacy, with the exception of language, is more powerful in facilitating one's personal transformational journey than that great chorus line of electrons, the one and only celebrated boxed idiot of our times, the television set.

SECOND PILLAR: **The grand stage for lunacy on television can be found in no better place than the culturally evolved _The Late Show with David Letterman_.** Letterman, a High Lunatic Wizard Extraordinaire, secretly has become the most important leader of American culture. The seriousness of top dollar politicians and business czars pales when contrasted to the powerful sword of lunacy held in the hands of Mr. Letterman. With the zap of a single one liner, a high tower of seriousness is toppled. My, oh my, this lunacy is really serious stuff!

THIRD PILLAR: The same power of lunacy that can expose the naked emptiness of an emperor's wardrobe is available as one of the most powerful instruments for self-transformation. **In the pages that follow, tasks, procedures, strategies, stagings, and recipes are prescribed that may radically alter the core of your being.** These extremely powerful doses of lunacy called "luna-cises," are radically dangerous to maintaining any addiction to the status quo, normality, and traditional definitions and attitudes toward success, happiness, and the meaning of life.

When these words were printed, a small miracle took place. David Letterman had a dream that he never knew he had. In this dream, Ed Sullivan told him the story you are now reading.

Although the ghost of Mr. Sullivan and the ghost of Socra-tease knew this to be so, David Letterman never knew he had that dream. All these things we know because it has been written that these things were said and that these things were done.

And now it's up to you, the owner of this manual of crazy wisdom and merriment, to do your part. It is you who are needed to bring even more magical life to *The Late Show* and, in turn, begin moving your life into a theatre of new possibilities and experiences.

So let's get on with the show, THE REALLY BIG SHOW!

(armadillo)

STOP!

Put this book down.

Do not read any further unless you are sitting this very moment in front of your TV watching the David Letterman Show. If you are unable to wait, then you may substitute the following task.

Say to yourself, right now:

"The David Letterman Show is a Really Big Show."

Put a bookmark on this page and excuse yourself to go find a very large piece of paper. Make certain it is large enough for your chair to sit upon. On this paper, use a marking pen to draw the outline of a large screen television set. On the screen, write these letters, "The David Letterman Show."

Place this on the floor, set your chair on the center of the screen, sit down, and proceed with the reading of this book.

No way around it, you're sitting inside a Really Big Shooow!

Living
with

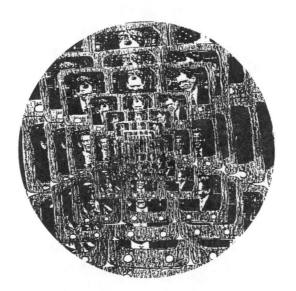

Letterman

GETTING TIGHT WITH DAVE

Watch the show this way

- Attach a piece of string to each of the four corners of your television set. The strings should be long enough to reach to where you sit when you watch the show.

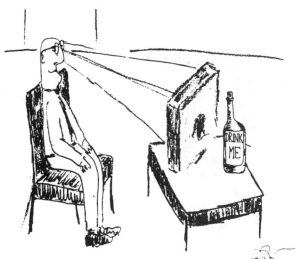

- Attach the other ends of the string to a pair of cheap sunglasses from which you have removed the lenses. Two strings will be attached to each side.

- When the show comes on, wear these glasses and move forward or backwards so that the four strings are as tight as possible.

Part by part!

- Stick the end of a string to a spot near the center of the screen.

- While watching Dave's monologue, hold the string in your hand and see how the attached end of the string moves from part to part over Dave's body as he moves.

- Move your end of the string to whatever part of your body matches. For example, if the end of the string is on top of Letterman's ear, move your end of the string to touch your ear.

- Try attaching several strings and having different people play at the same time. **Be careful, this is an adult game.**

THE LETTERMAN WATCHERS

- Have someone take many many photographs of you watching the David Letterman Show.

- When the photographs are developed, select shots of as many weird, funny, exaggerated but *real* reactions to Dave as you can find. (There should be closeups of your facial responses, whole body shots, and closeups of other body parts such as hands and feet.)

- Take these photos and rest them in a quiet place.

- An hour before the show, take out the photos and place them in the television viewing area. They are **The Watchers** come to watch the show. They are all the secret, unknown parts of yourself that want to watch the show along with you.

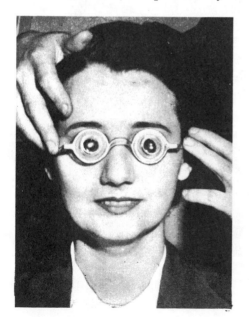

- At the end of the show, return them to their resting place. Repeat this procedure three times.

- After the Letterman Watchers have watched the show three times, attach them to large pieces of cardboard and store them in a closet. Only bring them out when Letterman has a guest you are super-excited about seeing. Otherwise, let your watchers rest in the dark.

One of the very few human beings who has actually been fitted for Giggle-goggles.

BE YOUR OWN TV

The watcher watching the watcher watch the watcher . . .

FINDING THE FUNNY SPOT

What is the funniest place in your house? Here's how to find out:

- For the next two weeks, watch the Letterman Show from a different place in your home every night. This will require moving the TV around the house. You may have to get a long cable cord. You will also need to buy some colored tape.

- Keep a log in which you rate the shows, making sure you write down *where you were in the house* when you viewed each one.

- At the end of two weeks, read over your log and decide which show was the funniest.

- Mark the spot. Obviously, this is the funniest place in your house. When you need a laugh, you know where to go.

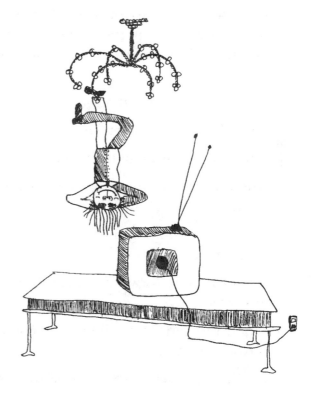

ALL ROADS LEAD TO LETTERMAN

- Either purchase or make a good supply of six-inch long direction pointers in the shape of arrows. A dozen of these will do.

- On the pointers, print, "D. L. SHOW."

- From every door and wall in your home, have the arrow pointers aimed toward your television set.

- Put up as many as you can.

- Every evening, just prior to showtime, travel along every pathway in your home and touch all the arrows pointing to the show. If there are other people also watching, make it a race to see who can be first to touch all the Letterman road signs.

- As you run through the race course, shout out, "**All roads lead to Letterman!**"

- Run this race for seven shows. After the seventh race, take the arrows down.

- Glue the arrows together, one on top of another, to create one thick arrow.

- Using a string, hang this arrow from your ceiling over the television set for another seven shows.

- When that hanging time is complete, take the arrow down and find a special place for it.

- From that day forward, always bring out the "D. L." arrow before you watch the show.

- When the Letterman Show first comes on the air, touch the screen with the arrow's point.

- Do this for every Letterman show you watch.

THERE ARE NO OTHER SHORTCUTS TO HAPPINESS.

INVITE YOUR NEIGHBORS' LAWNMOWERS OVER TO WATCH THE SHOW

- Tell your neighbors that you want to videotape their mowers enjoying David Letterman. Tell them that if enough lawnmowers show up, they might actually get on the real Letterman show.

- Arrange to have a neighborhood meeting to discuss creative ways of staging this event. For instance, the mowers might want some refreshments, so you will have to solicit requests!

Make this absolutely the wackiest event that ever took place on your block.

- **Send the videotape to Dave and to your local TV station.***

*If you send one to us, we may include it in the collection "Great Mower Moments with Letterman" or its sequel "More Mower Moments."

LETTERMAN COVER-UP

- Obtain a piece of cardboard the size of your TV screen.

- In the middle of this cardboard make a hole that is the typical size of David Letterman's head as it is seen on your screen.

- At the beginning of the show, place the circle over the part of the screen where Dave's head usually appears during his stand-up monologue.

- Watch the monologue through the cut-out circle, allowing only Letterman's head to be seen.

- Let your mind run wild, imaginging what is really happening behind the "cover-up."

LETTERMAN, THE SHAPE SHIFTER

• Cut out photos (or drawings) of the heads of at least a dozen different kinds of animals. (The size of the animal heads should be about the same size as Dave's head appears on your TV screen.)

• Acquire a dozen dowel sticks one third of an inch in diameter and about two feet long and glue the photos to the ends of the sticks.

• If the show ever lapses into a dull spot, pull out your animal collection and hold the animal heads over Dave's head as he talks. Watch Dave "shape-shift" into the different creatures.

• Invite people over to watch these miraculous transformations.

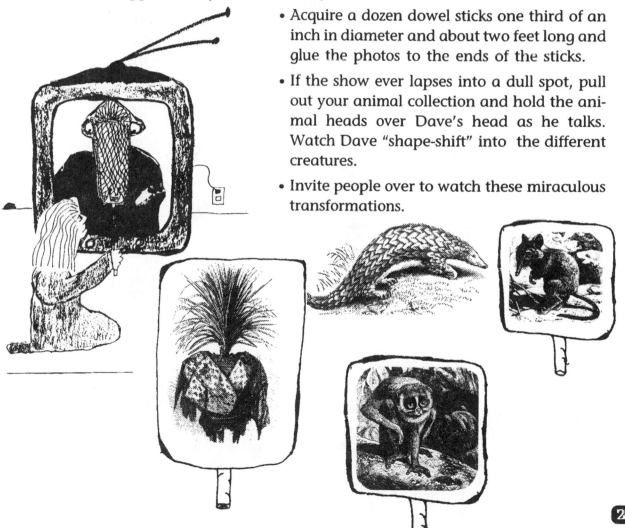

DRESSING UP FOR DAVE

Open up your closets and get ready. This one will take some effort.

- As you watch the show, you are to change clothes every time there is a commercial break. Begin with your most formal attire. Then proceed changing into every outfit you have until the show is over. If you run out of clothes, repeat with previously worn outfits. If you don't get through your wardrobe, continue the next evening and subsequent evenings until you've shown Dave every stitch of clothing you've got.

It's 11:30 — Do you know where your costumes are?

THE HILLS ARE ALIVE ...

- Gather all the buzzers, beepers, bike horns, bull horns, bugles, tweeters, snappers, poppers, and drums that you can find.

- At Letterman time, round up your friends, enemies, in-laws, animals, employers, employees, and offspring. Distribute this collection of auditory gadgets to everyone come who may.

- Turn up the volume of your television and let the sounds fly.

- Experiment with different ways of using your sound makers to express your reaction to the show. For instance, you might make a particularly raucous sound whenever Dave comes out with one of the following:

  Nice to see you! You look great! Do you get to New York much? I don't mean to sound like a dweeb but . . .

Distant cousin of the author who's been trying to land a job as Letterman's sound effects technician since the show came on the air.

Throw the bum out . . .

- Purchase a supply of cheap, red, colored paper.

- Crumple the paper into wadded balls and put them in a basket.

- Invite some friends over to watch a Letterman show. Explain that you have always envied vaudeville audiences who threw tomatoes at bad performers. Show them your basket of red paper tomatoes and invite them to do the same when there is a dull moment on the show.

- Videotape yourself and your friends watching the show and letting the tomatoes fly.

- Don't throw them unless you're really moved to do so.

You might also want to have a basket of eggs — wads of *yellow*, colored paper.

An experienced recipient of multiple tomato and egg dousings, this Vaudeville performer invented a device for creating a real cat out of an imaginary balloon.

or . . . blame it on the *DUD GUN!*

There is an alternative approach to this assignment that I personally recommend. If you do not want to dirty Dave's wardrobe and are as loyal to him as you ought to be, then do the following variation. When the show has a dull moment, blame it on another talk show host on another network. Quickly turn to the other channel and launch the produce.

Presume that the other network is envious of all the talented people that are on the Letterman staff. This other network subsequently hired highly intelligent former defense research scientists to attack the show. The evil plot they conspired revolves around a top secret

Dud Gun.

Dud gun used by saboteurs from hostile networks to make Dave's jokes go bad.

It zaps the humor right out of the show. This conspiracy is so secret and so unimaginable that even *The National Enquirer* knows nothing about it.

As you now watch the Letterman show, be on the lookout for the sinister workings of the "Dud Gun." When you see a fizzled moment, shout out, "Dud Gun," turn to that other network, and attack. This is the only way to stop these network dirty tricks. When word gets out that produce is being thrown at these other shows, the scientists will lose their contracts. In their anger they will turn on the networks that hired them and spray them with one final lethal dose of dudness.

THE LETTERMAN FROM OUTER SPACE

It is possible that David Letterman is an alien from a friendly, but foreign planet. He has been sent to our world to prevent the seriousness now infecting us from getting any worse. If things don't stop getting *heavier,* surely we are doomed.

Letterman is here to beam hilarity waves into our minds.

As you watch him carefully note how, from time to time, Dave does something unusual with his eyes. These are moments when he is sending the interplanetary treatment our way. Sometimes he's obvious about it and at other times he sneaks it in. Watch for this the next time you watch the show and you will see exactly what I'm talking about.

Now that you know it is possible that he really is sending us some kind of treatment during the show, prepare yourself to receive the beam. The next time you and your friends watch the show, study Dave's eyes. The moment someone notices a difference in how they are looking at you, tell the group, "He's beaming us."

At that moment, everyone is to get completely weird and act wild and crazy, but only for three seconds. You don't want to miss another treatment.

It's extremely important that people begin receiving this treatment. If Dave's superiors begin noticing that no one is noticing, they may take more drastic measures to correct our situation. Let's not take any chances. Look into his eyes and allow the force to hit you right smack in your transformational center.

ALIENS HAVE DECIDED TO BE FRIENDLY TO LATE NIGHTERS.

"He's beaming us!"

SUBLIME RECEPTION

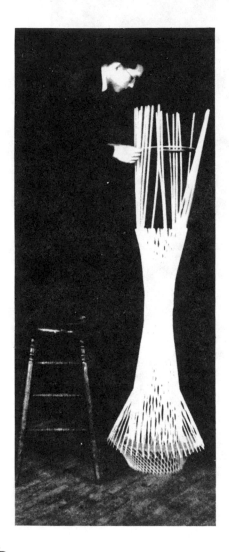

Alternative Letterman antenna made with soda straws (and toothpicks forming the joints.)

- Build an antenna made of pencils.

- Attach the pencils together in any way you can think of and build a tower. You may follow any design you desire. Make certain the bottom pencil(s) have been sharpened.

- Set this antenna next to your television set.

- Connect the television to the antenna by using a string.

- Think: this antenna brings in additional information from the Letterman Show I previously wasn't able to receive.

- As you watch the show with this new antenna, make a list of things you didn't notice about the show before.

- Attribute these new awarenesses to the enhanced reception brought about by the antenna of pencils.

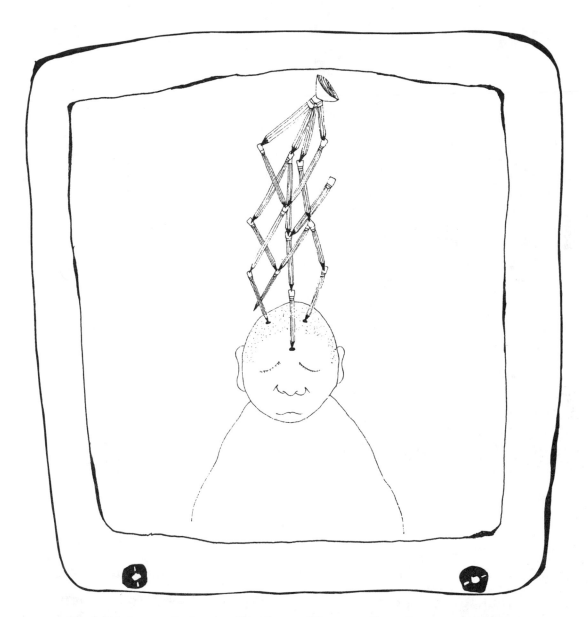

Buddhist monk in meditation with pencil antennae implants.

EYES SPY

Camouflaged as a Christmas tree, this seasoned Letterfreak spies on his own TV set.

- Watch the Letterman Show with binoculars.

- Move around to learn what can be learned by watching the show this way.

- Do this for five minutes during every show for a week.

- The following week, hook up two tin cans to a long piece of string to make the kind of "phone" children make in elementary science class.

- When Letterman is on, have someone hold one can over the television speaker. Stretch the string so it is tight and place the other can over your ear. Get as far away as you can to listen in this way.

- Practice doing this for five minutes a show throughout the next week.

- Now put the "binocular viewing" and the "tin can listening" together.

- For five minutes, coordinate this arrangement with a friend. Take turns helping one another do it.

When you think you've figured out how to do it smoothly, invite someone over who doesn't know about this peculiar arrangement. When the show comes on, proceed to set up the cans and binoculars. Without a smile, act as if you know what you are doing. Make expressions of amazement when you listen and observe in this alternative set up. Ask the invited guest if he or she wants to learn to really see the show. You and your accomplice are then to do your best to teach this person how to listen with a tin can and see through a pair of binoculars.

Ancient auditor attempting to listen in on his own thoughts.

Our man in Vaudeville receiving information from everywhere.

Binocular watching and tin-can listening at the same time.

THE REAL SHOW

- Set your TV up in a private room, such as the bedroom.

- Invite as many friends and family members to participate in this exercise as you can. You'll need a TV that can be connected to an audio head-set and a VCR.

- Choose one person to be the Designated Observer (D.O.). Only she or he is to watch the show, turning the speaker off and listening with the head-set so no one else can hear what is going on.

- Use the VCR to tape the show.

- Choose another person to be an Informant, planted just outside the room where the TV is.

- Choose a third person to be the Runner, standing next to the Informant.

- Choose a fourth person to be an Interpreter, positioned in a room as far as possible from the TV room.

- The rest of the guests should wait in the same room as the Interpreter.

- As the D.O. watches the show, he or she must report out loud what is happening on it to the informant.

- Upon hearing this, the informant must write what he or she hears on index cards.

- These cards are then carried by the runner to the distant room.

- Here the interpreter, using the cards as a source of information, tells the rest of the guests what has been happening on the show.

- The runner now returns to the TV room to pick up the next message from the informant.

- This process should continue throughout the show.

- After the show is over, invite everyone back to the TV room and play the tape. Beware! You may be driven mad with laughter at how wildly the Interpreter's report strays from the **real show**.

- If you can't muster a big crowd for this exercise, here's a variation: Communicate what's happening from room to room via "tin-can-telephones."

RED LIGHT DISTRACT

- Purchase a red light and mount it over the door to the room where you watch the Letterman Show.

- When it's showtime, turn on the red light and tell everyone to be quiet because you want to be in a "live" show. (Never use the light except when Letterman is on.)

- If and only if you have set up this red light and watched at least thirteen shows under its rays, you may consider yourself a **Big Time Letterman Fan**.

KEYS TO COUNT ON

- Count the number of keyboards in Paul Shaffer's band.

- Give a code name to each keyboard, and over the weeks keep count of how often he uses each one.

- After several months, send Paul a letter and give him a report. Ask him why the camera only showed him playing the keyboard on top of the acoustic piano a total of, say, three times in the last three months.

Paul Shaffer's former understudy . . .   *and future understudy*

- Request that he ask the show's director to allow more time for seeing those keyboards.

WE, THE VIEWERS, WANT TO KNOW MORE ABOUT THOSE KEYS. How many cables are used to hook up all that equipment? What color are they? Is Paul an electrical engineer? Is he insured in case he is electrically shocked by his instrument? How many keyboards does he have at home? Which one does he like to play the most? Does David Letterman allow him to play that one more often than the others? **We want more information about that musical space station Paul Shaffer hides out in.**

LETTERMAN CROSSES THE DELAWARE

- Find some magazines that have photographs of David Letterman.

- Gather pictures or illustrations of famous historical scenes — George Washington crossing the Delaware, the first man on the moon, Babe Ruth's famous home run, and so forth.

- Tape or glue photographs of Dave's head on to these images so that Dave appears to be part of the scene.

- Do the same with images of yourself and your friends.

- Place this gallery of historically important scenes on the wall behind your television set.

AND NOW IT'S TIME FOR A BEDTIME STORY

There was once a potato who was given a television set that only received the image of David Letterman. This spud spent an entire lifetime staring at Mr. Letterman, believing Dave was a map of the world beyond his small plot of soil.

When the potato was finally eaten, it went to potato heaven and faced the God of all Vegetables. This diety asked our Letterman spud what he had learned in a lifetime. The potato spoke for the first time:

"I learned that all letters belong to man."

God then asked if he understood why he had spent a lifetime staring at a television screen. The potato paused and said, "I think it was some kind of preparation." God smiled and replied, "Yes, my spud, your eyes have seen some truth. It is now time to let you know about what the vegetables do for the two leggeds called human beings."

Our devoted tuber was taken to a great hall of roots where all the secret knowledge of vegetation was whipped into his being. All we are permitted to say at this point is that he was given the task of helping you see into the dream world of David Letterman. This is the place where all seeds of lunacy and humor are born.

He learned how delivering these seeds of sweet madness to human beings requires an image, a dream image, so that it may be germinated. Our potato, now an angel of vegetation, has been so kind as to have delivered to us dream images from the dream world of David Letterman. Although Dave may have never consciously seen these images, they are from the deep well of imagination that feeds his whole being.

At this time you will see some of Dave's dreams. Underneath each image is a dream interpretation by a former psychoanalyst who is now an assistant to the potato people. He is presently known as Dr. Sigmund Fraud. His words have been provided to help give you a glimpse of the truth conveyed by each of these dream images.

There is no end to this story. Its only purpose was bringing us to Dave's Dreams. . .

DAVE IS DREAMING THAT . . .

. . . this aged technician and his strange machine are really the secret sources of all Letterman shows.

. . . *he's a foundling from outer space.*

. . . *a highly advanced form of television*
consciousness has finally arrived.

. . . *he's up for that famous screen test*
all over again.

Exercises

for developing a
Letterman
State of

Mind

VOLUNTARY MULTIPLES

- For the next seven days call your own answering machine and leave yourself this message: "I can have several personalities if I want." Do this twice a day.
- Try using many different voices and speaking styles when you leave each message.

WHEN TWO PENS ARE BETTER THAN ONE

- Tape two pens together.
- Carry this and a note pad with you when you are at work. In the presence of someone you think is too serious, pull out the pen and pretend to write down something important. You are actually to write this pre-planned message:

I'm being treated for over-seriousness.
I'm being treated for over-seriousness.
Thank you for your concern.
Thank you for your concern.

- Whenever the serious person asks you why you have two pens attached together, immediately give the person your "double message" and say, "Because this message is for two people — you and me." If you are asked to give a further explanation of the message, simply say, "I had to write what had already been written. You see, this is a 'double message.'"

- If the person does not ask these questions, obviously they weren't serious enough! Go out and try again!

THE NOSE IS THE BRAIN OF HUMOR

- Draw your profile on a piece of paper, enlisting the help of a friend if necessary.

- Draw an outline around that profile that is twice as large. In this way, you are to imagine you have expanded your mind.

- Make another outline, expanding your mind even more.

- Do this until you have at least half a dozen minds, with the last one covering most of the floor space of the room you're using for this exercise.

- Do not color or write upon the inside of your first mind. Keep this one empty.

- For the next level of mind expansion, write down the name of everyone in your family of origin you have ever met, whether they are presently alive or not.

- For the next level of mind, write down the names of your friends, colleagues, and neighbors.

- On the subsequent level, place your phonebook within the outline and put your phone on top of it. Think of this level of mind as your link with everyone else in the world.

- Fill in the other mind levels with whatever you want, saving the last two levels for the following placements.

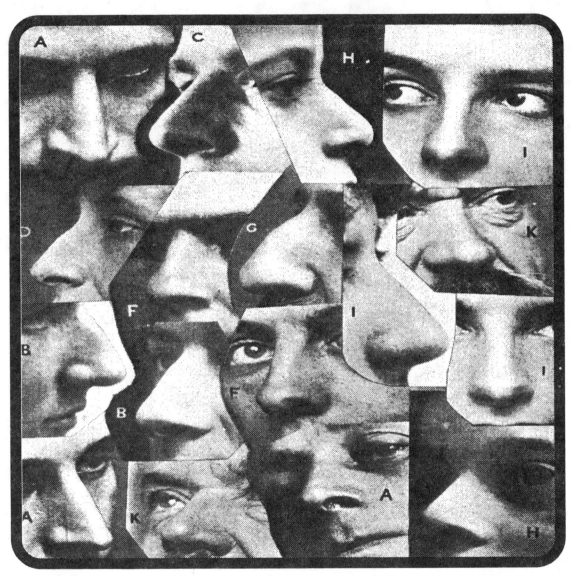 **CERTIFIED NOSES**

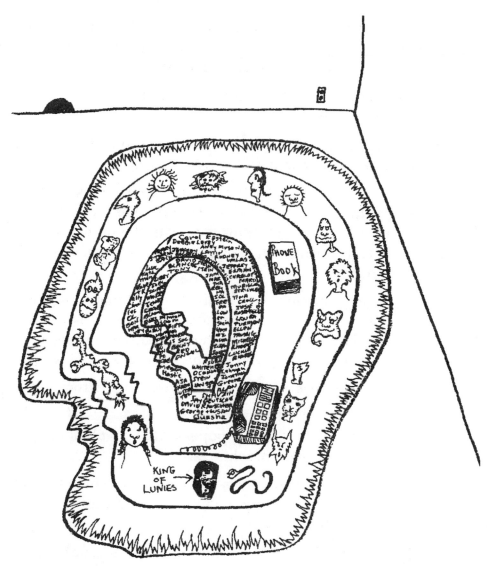

Mind expansion diagram

- On the next to last level, place photographs of silly faces and funny expressions taken of animals. In this ring draw your own picture of David Letterman as a stick man with the caption, **King of Lunies.**

- On the last level, fill it with many colors, making certain that its outermost circumference is left white.

- Stand on top of the middle of the first outline you drew, that is, your empty head. Be mindful of what your nose looks like.

- Walk to the next level and consider the noses of your family members, then proceed to consider the noses of everyone else on other levels. When you get to Letterman, kneel down and touch his nose with the tip of your left elbow, saying the following piece of nonsense, as if it were an eternal verity, "The nose is the brain of humor."

- When you have walked through these many levels of mind, step outside the room and look at the outlines from the perspective of standing outside the door looking in. Play back in your mind what it would have looked like if you had been someone else watching you do this exercise.

- Say to yourself, "It is always nosy to watch your mind from outside your mind."

- Go back into the room and fold up the paperwork. Fold all of the paper into a pile and tie it up with a piece of white string.

- Mail this pile of mind to a friend who is addicted to watching the Letterman show and attach a note: "Here's a piece of mind. See if your mind can figure this out. It has to do with Letterman."

- Make certain you save a little piece of these minds for yourself.

Meditation
on The Life-Cycle of a Laugh

- While watching Letterman, hold an egg in each hand.
- Think of each burst of laughter you hear on the show as being the sound of a tiny birth of humor.
- Now hold an apple in one hand and an orange in the other.

- Think of how healthy fruits are for the body and the mind.
- Do each of the above exercises for five minutes.

- For the next minute hold a head of lettuce on top of your head and consider how Letterman lets us really encounter lunacy.
- Finally, hold one drop of water on the bridge of your nose for three seconds.
- Meditate on what the world would be like if we were all drowning in laughter.

THE MUMMY AT THE CENTER OF IT ALL

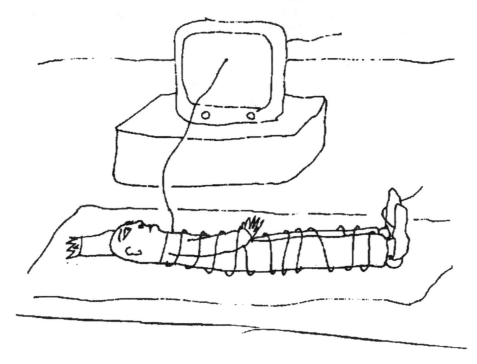

- Tape one end of a ball of string to the center of your viewing screen.

- Call that center point *the navel of the broadcast.*

- Extend the length of string to the area where you sit and watch television.

- Wrap the rest of your body with the string, making yourself a partial mummy.

- Watch the Letterman show while you are connected to the center in this way.

HOW DAVE PREPARES TO GO ON THE AIR

- Find a nice tall tree with lawn space around it.
- Carefully attach to the tree a big drawing of an eye.
- Sit in front of a tree in the lawn chair and stare at the tree's eye for five minutes.
- Next, remove the eye from the tree and tape a piece of string to it so you can wear it as a mask.
- Punch two holes in the eye so you can see through it.
- Sit in your chair and stare at the tree through its eye.
- Imagine that David Letterman does this every day as a means of preparing for his show.

BAPTIZING THE EARTH
WITH THE WATERS OF LUNACY

- Fill a canteen with water and set it on top of the television while the Letterman Show is on.

- The next day go to a public park searching for a dry spot of ground that needs a drink.

- Provide it with water and say to the ground, "Here's some water radiated by the Letterman Show."

- Return home immediately and meditate on how you baptized the earth with lunacy.

JUST DESERTS

As a reward for perservering in your quest for hilarity, here is your lunacy gift certificate:

LUNACY GIFT CERTIFICATE

This certificate officially grants you permission to have one minute of absolute lunacy in your life. At this very instant you are to hop up in the air twelve times. When you hop, say outloud, "Let this hop be my top and may my top enjoy the hop." If anyone is watching, tell them you suffer from a serious addiction to seriousness and that you're participating in an experimental "Twelve Hops" treatment program. Mention that your full recovery requires dedication to preparing yourself for the David Letterman Show.

Twelve-hoppers in the bliss of recovery.

ADOPT A LETTER FOR A DAY

Choose one letter from the alphabet. Adopt it for the day. While carrying this book, introduce your alphabet letter to your friends by reading them this message:

I know this is going to sound weird, but there is a lunatic assignment I took a pledge to perform. It involves me reading this introduction to you this very moment. All I am going to do is introduce you to a letter I've adopted for today. It's name is ____ (fill in with the letter chosen). This assignment has something to do with helping me develop the kind of mind that will have an enhanced ability to appreciate the David Letterman Show. That's all I have to read. Thanks for participating in this small moment of lunacy.

Two Letter-persons introducing their letters to each other.

ALL THE PROPHETS KNEW THIS BOOK WAS COMING.

THE REASONS WHY

- Open up the phone book and choose someone's name at random.

- Sit down and write that person a letter.

- Give them three reasons why they should become more serious about adding some humor to their life.

- In addition, create the most ridiculous reason you can think of why they should watch the David Letterman Show.

- Sign the letter, put it in an envelope, and address it.

- Throw it away in the wastebasket of a post office.

NOTHING NEW UNDER THE SUN

- Go to your public library and make a copy of the weather forecast given for this day ten years ago.

- Do this every day until you find a weather forecast for that day ten years before that is accurate for the present weather situation.

- On such a day, tell at least three people that nothing has changed in ten years.

- Show them the forecast that was made ten years ago to prove your point.

DON'T LAUGH AT THIS JOKE

- Go to a novelty shop, purchase the silliest little thing you can find, and locate a box to place it in.

- Put a message on the cover of the box that states, "Please open and do not smile. If you smile, it must be given away to someone else."

- Leave this box in the dressing room of a clothing store.

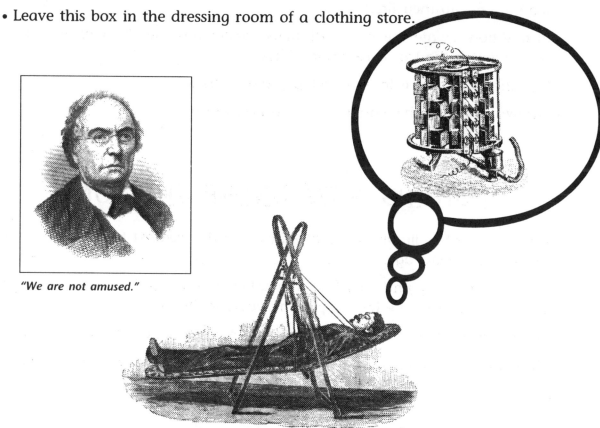

"We are not amused."

Letterman fan, attempting to become a grasshopper, dreams of a strange device

FAST FOOD FAST

- Go to a fast food restaurant you believe is selling food that is not appropriately nutritious for children. Find a picture in a magazine of the kind of meal they should be eating. Invade the restaurant and indiscretely place these subversive photos in strategic locations like in the napkin dispensers or by the straw machine or next to the cash register or under the giveaways! If the manager asks what you're doing — **RUN FOR IT!**

CARD BARDS

- On Father's Day purchase a Father's Day card. Hold onto the card and mail it to your mother on Halloween. Inside the card write, "Happy Thanksgiving!"

- On Halloween purchase a birthday card. Give it to your friend on the Fourth of July with the instructions to send it to you on your birthday.

This woman took her TV apart and found that it contained a device to aid in the selection of greeting cards. (The above two lunacises are examples of her work.)

THIS WAS WRITTEN BECAUSE YOU DESERVE TO KNOW EVERYTHING.

THE CONSCIOUS BIRTH OF A MAD IDEA

- Purchase the tiniest light bulb you can find. Hold it in your hand and take a fifteen minute walk.

- Do this every day until you get a great idea for prescribing some lunacy. It should make you laugh outloud.

- When that happens, replace the lightbulb and repeat the procedure.

- Schedule this activity into your life on a regular basis to keep your lunacy in good shape.

GALLERY OF SERIOUS PERSONS
& ENLIGHTENED ONES

Which is who?
(Only the enlightened know for sure.)

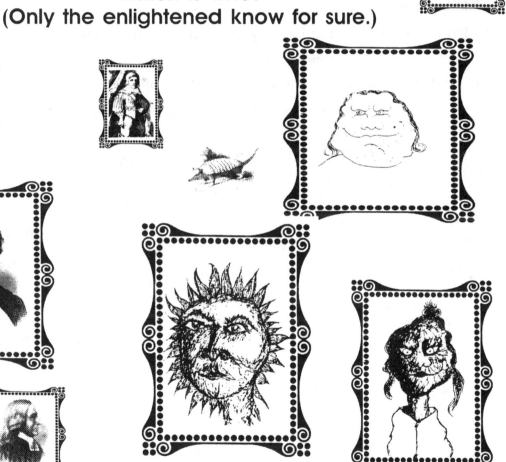

(on loan
to the
Louvre)

MONA LISA

STANDING ROOM ONLY

- Have a sign made that proclaims: "NO SITTING."

- Conduct this experiment: place this sign in different spots in your house and determine where it brings forth the most humor.

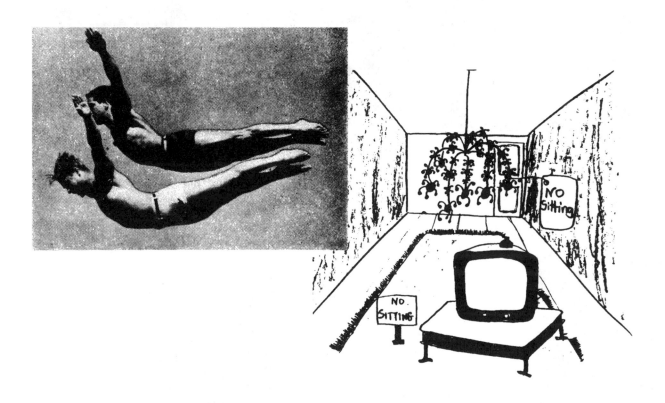

GETTING THE POINT

- Using a pen with an extremely fine point, put a dot on the tip of your nose. It should not be noticeable by anyone unless they are standing very close to you.

- Go through a day and think about how it is often difficult to make a point that other people notice.

- If anyone does notice and says something, ask them whether they believe anyone else will notice the point on your nose. If they say no, then say, "That's the whole point."

WORLD-CLASS PROPELLER BEANIE

- Purchase a beanie with a propeller that has four blades on the top of it and a small magnetic compass.

- Attach a piece of string to each of the blades so that they may line up with the four directions of space — north, south, east, and west.

- Put on your beanie and take your seat in the center of the room.

- Have a friend attach the ends of all four strings to the walls so that a line of string extends in each of the four directions.

- Hold the compass in your hand and feel how you and the compass are one.

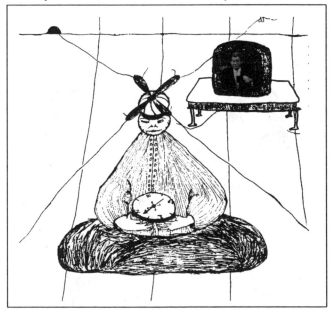

Person contemplating the four directions of space with magnetic compass and propeller beanie (made rigid by strings.)

THE ENDLESS LETTERMAN

- Cut out as many pictures of David Letterman as you can find.

- Make copies and tape them to little pieces of cardboard so the pictures will stand up.

- Make a collection of one hundred of these miniature Lettermans.

- Line them up in rows in front of your television and allow them to watch their favorite show.

NO - BRAINER

- Go to the library and, using a copy machine, copy pictures of the brains of many animals — bird brains, monkey brains, donkey brains, whale brains, and so forth.

- Place one of these brains on top of your head as you watch the Letterman Show.

- Meditate on what it would be like to watch the show if you were a bird, a monkey, a donkey, etc.

- Try out every brain in your collection.

(armadillo)

Extragalactic brain

Fossilized brain of Topo Gigio, frequent guest on the old Ed Sullivan Show, recovered from a rusted mouse trap in the basement of the Sullivan Theater.

Man and woman, wielding animal brain placards, enjoy Late Show.

Enhanced sonogram of Letterman gag-writer "luminescing" with bright ideas.

Quayle brain

SUPERMAN IN A SHOE BOX

- Place a doll or cut-out picture of superman in a shoe box.

- Take this shoe box to a phone booth within viewing distance of a sidewalk cafe or restaurant.

- Write on top of the shoe box, "Help! Please open."

- Have the following note attached to the superman in the shoe box:

Thank you for opening the box. As you can see, I am superman. Unfortunately, I got myself stuck in another dimension. I figured if I left this solidified hologram in a phone booth, the person finding it will know it is really me. I need you to hold me over your head and spin around three times. Then place me back into the shoe box. When you have done this, proceed to open the letter that is placed inside the phone book of this booth.

You need to have placed a note inside the phone book saying:

Interactive Questionnaire

1. If you believe you are on Candid Camera *then wave to the audience this very moment.*

2. If you believe you are being taped for the Late Show *then jump up and down.*

Thank you for your cooperation. Remember, humor is good for your health and food for your soul. Enclosed is five dollars. Please purchase something silly and leave it in another phone booth. Remember to attach a goofy letter.

Sincerely yours,

Someone who hopes you watch all future Letterman shows

DOUBLE IN-SIGHT

- Obtain two cardboard boxes the size of your television set.

- On one side of each box cut out an area to be your "screen." With marking pens, draw in television knobs for channel selection, volume, and other adjustments.

- Wear this cardboard television set over your head when you watch Letterman so that your head will appear on this screen.

- Do this with a friend who will also be wearing a television "headset."

- Only wear these televisions when you watch Letterman.

- Find out how many double in-sights you can create. (The first double in-sight will arise as a shared understanding of what the term, "double in-sight," is supposed to mean. For a hint, examine the next page.)

IN A RUT OR IN THE GROOVE?

- Place two TVs together, back to back. (If you can, add two other sets, one on each side.)

- Place the televisions on the floor and get on all fours.

- With a group of at least two people, crawl around these four sets at different speeds as you watch the Letterman Show.

- See if you can notice any repetitive patterns in your movement. For instance, do you speed up or slow down when the show really gets moving? When the talk show talk slows down, do you?

- Learn how to get in rhythm with the pace of the show.

The Practice of Weirdness

Once upon a time, a very special person read a book called *The Lunatic Guide to the David Letterman Show* and came to a story titled, "The Practice of Weirdness." When the person read this story, it said the very same thing you are presently reading. It went on to say that this tale will be more than a story and will include some weird things to do.

In this story, the main character just happened to have the same name as you. This person, whom we identify as W.P. (weird person), woke up one day to find the following message written on a piece of paper attached to the inside of a shoe:

The next time you watch The David Letterman Show *bring along a pen and a stack of paper. When the show begins, write down all the things you enjoy in the world. You are to pretend that this is like a free shopping spree where everything you select while the show is on the air will actually be given to you. Your list might include your favorite foods, books, places to travel, games, experiences, friends, and so forth. Do this part of the assignment in order to find out what will happen next.*

On that very evening *The David Letterman Show* was scheduled to be broadcast. Following the instructions, W.P. made a list of all the enjoyable things that could be imagined. The next morning W.P. woke up and found a cork floating on top of the room's aquarium. Lifting this cork out of the water, W.P. found a message written on it:

Choose the top three things you enjoy the most that are written on your list. Do this before you go to sleep tonight. Place this list beneath your bed, directly under your head. Further instructions to follow.

Prior to retiring for the night, W.P. wrote down these three favorite things and placed the list underneath the bed in the prescribed manner. In the middle of the night W.P. was awakened by the sound of a bird whistling. When (s)he turned on the room light, no bird could be found. When (s)he turned the light off, the whistling returned. Rather than continue trying to see the bird, W.P. decided to listen very carefully to its song. The bird's song did not put W.P. to sleep. It made W.P. start singing along with the bird.

As W.P. began singing with this bird, the bird began talking and, to W.P.'s great surprise, W.P. spoke the same words at the same time. These are the words that were heard in the room:

"Pull out the List of the three favorite things that is underneath the bed. With a pencil, scratch out the second and third items and only leave the first item. Neatly fold this paper three times and place it under you pillow. Rest your head on the pillow for five minutes and then get up, removing the paper. You will then find out what will happen."

W.P. faithfully did this and after five minutes of resting his head on top of the name of the one remaining enjoyable thing, he arose and said, "What now? How much more do I have to do?"

A different voice was heard outside the room. Going to the window, W.P. looked into the sky and heard these words spoken, "Congratulations W.P. You have passed the weirdness test. We can now teach you how to do some advanced weirdness. Tomorrow morning you will receive your instructions in the mail box."

It should not be a surprise that W.P. did not sleep for the rest of that night. W.P. could not stop thinking about the weirdness that had entered his life. When the sun came up that next morning, W.P. ran out to the mailbox to see if there was an envelope with the promised instructions.

Inside the mailbox was a large brown envelope with the initials W.P. written on it.

W.P. tore it open and found another envelope, this one colored blue and black. Inside the second envelope was a message:

"Write down the weirdest thing you can think of doing with a paper clip. Place these instructions inside a book in your public library and check the mailbox the following day."

W.P. had gone too far to turn back now. A weird task involving a paper clip was created. To the best of my memory, W.P. came up with these instructions:

Take a box of paper clips and go to the center of your town. Link the paper clips and line them up creating a single straight line from the town center in whatever direction you choose. Mark the end of this line with a stone. Sit and guard this stone for thirty minutes. When the time is up, remove the stone and pick up the paper clips. Bring them home with you and place them in a shoebox. Label this box, "artifacts of a weird moment." Keep this box in a safe place.

The following day W.P. found a note in the mailbox that praised the weird task. The note gave the exact measurement of each paper clip and provided more instructions. These instructions had something to do with completing one final task:

You are to write one thousand weird assignments to be sprinkled throughout your travels and journeys. They are to be weird, bizarre, nonsensical, mysterious, and strange. When you finish spreading these seeds of weirdness, send a letter to the Postmaster of the South Pole saying, "It is done."

Years later a letter arrived at W.P.'s mailbox. The letter congratulated W.P. for completing the last assignment. It told W.P. to come to the South Pole where the meaning of this exercise would be found.

As amazing as it sounds, W.P. actually organized a polar expedition and went to the bottom of the world. On the exact spot where the south pole exists, a penguin was standing with a black pouch around its waist. W.P. took the pouch, opened it up, and read the following message:

The story you are reading is guaranteed to weed out anyone who does not have a talent for creating weirdness and magic and mystery. Those people would not get this far in the story. For everyone else, it can now be stated that you are an official W.P. You have a job to do and this is what must be accomplished:

1. Choose three weird tasks in this book, whether in this story or in another part of the Lunatic Guide. Do the tasks.

2. Wait one week after doing these three weird things. At the end of that week, begin inventing and writing down one weird assignment for every day. Keep doing this until you have a collection of ten weird assignments.

3. At the end of completing ten weird assignments, purchase a world map and place it on your bedroom wall. Mark the spot where you live with a red marking pen. Measure one inch south from that spot and mark it with the pen.

4. After every ten weird assignments that you invent and write down, measure another inch below the last spot. Continue doing this until you have reached the south pole on your map.

5. When you reach the South Pole throw yourself a party celebrating your achievement. Use a lot of ice for this party and announce a competition among your friends to reach the North Pole. You may break up into expedition teams or do solo journeys. Everyone is to get into the weirdness and keep charting the journey to the top of the world.

It is important that you know that I have been to both the North and South Poles without leaving my own backyard. That's only part of the mysterious magic that comes from practicing weirdness!

LUNACY BREAK

- Take five minutes off every day to devote your attention to lunacy.

- Call this time your **lunacy break.**

- During your lunacy break stand in front of a mirror and make funny faces.

- Imagine that the mirror is a one-way mirror and that David Letterman is watching from the other side.

DAVE IS DREAMING ....

INTERPRETATION i: *No amount of money or persuasion will be able to get this world-champion fly swatter on to the show.*

INTERPRETATION II: *Heeere's Johnny . . .*

. . . of appeasing the spectre of the Bleepmaster.

...OF STUPID HUMAN TRICKS TO COME.

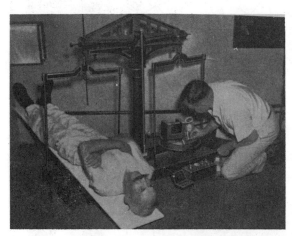

Old man levitates having laughed his weight away.

What goes up . . .

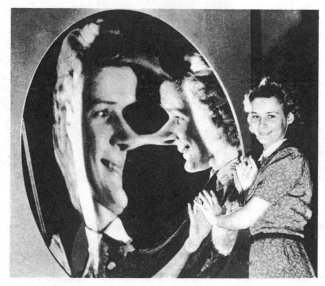

This debutante uses Silly Putty to give herself a nose job.

Around the World

with

Dave

ATTENTION: BIRDS AND CROCODILES

- Find out how to contact a crocodile farm in Australia.

- Call, write, or fax this place, saying you're an American interested in finding an interesting story.

- Politely ask them to tell you their favorite crocodile story.

Dweebodile

- Send this story to three bird sanctuaries in the United States.

- Ask them what they think of the story.

- If no one responds, call them and ask for the names of other bird sanctuaries they think might respond. You can tell them that this is a research project for a major television network.

- When a bird sanctuary does respond, thank them and ask them for their favorite bird story.

- Send the bird story to the Australian crocodile farm and ask them what they think.

- Send your results to the Letterman Show. On the envelope's address write, "Attention: Birds and Crocodiles." They will know what is coming their way.

... AND HE WENT DWEEB, DWEEB, DWEEB ALL THE WAY HOME.

ONE WORLD

- Purchase a small children's globe. (Get the inexpensive kind you find in a toy store.)

- As you watch Letterman,

    1. spin the globe everytime he introduces a guest,

    2. throw it up in the air and catch it when the guest sits down, and

    3. roll the globe back and forth during commercial breaks.

Over time the surface area of your globe should begin wearing down. You may want to speed up the process by using sandpaper on it whenever Letterman reads a Top Ten List. As you wear out the surface, notice how no country is distinct anymore. The whole world no longer has the arbitrary boundaries that over-serious humanoids believe mark off separate countries. Meditate on how watching Letterman helps make the world one place.

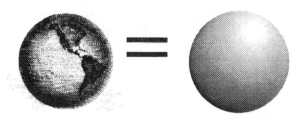

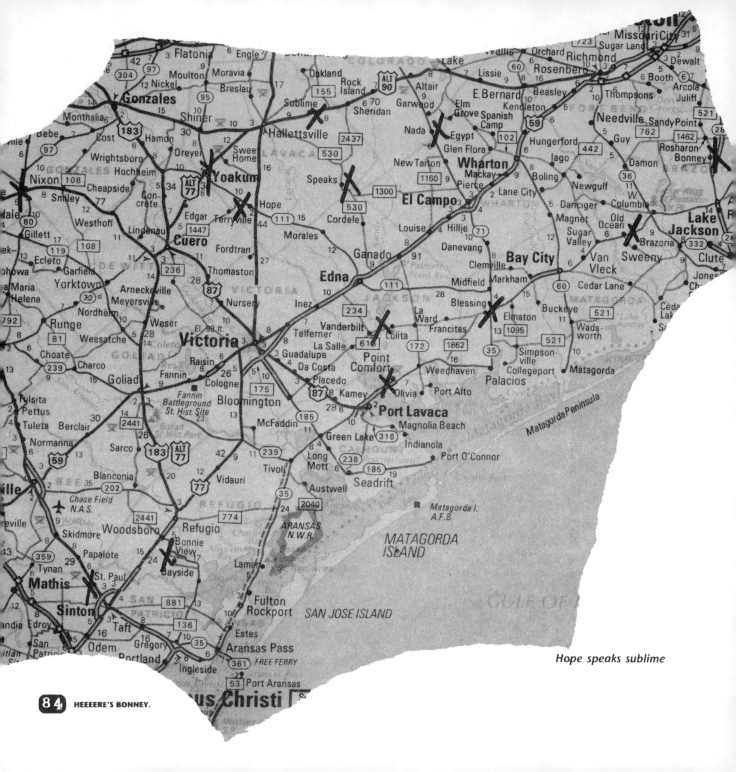

Hope speaks sublime

HOPSCOTCHING THE WORLD FOR WEIRDNESS

Keep a record of the times you watch Letterman. Do this in the following most unusual way:

- Obtain a compass and a map of the United States. Each day choose a place from which to imagine watching the show that evening.

- Go to an encyclopedia or reference book at the library and find out three things about that place.

- Write these interesting facts down and tell at least three people about this city during the day.

- Before the show comes on, take out your compass and, to the best of your ability, make the TV face in the direction of the location you chose. Rearrange the room to accommodate this fixing of coordinates.

- After the show, place a red "X" on the map to indicate you've watched it from that spot.

- Call up one of the three people you spoke to earlier and tell them how you enjoyed watching the show from this part of the country.

- Work yourself around the nation in the evenings to come.

LATE NIGHT LETTERFISH I

- Obtain an aquarium that is as large as your television screen.

- Put this aquarium directly in front of the television so you can only see the screen by looking through the glass.

- Fill the aquarium with water and add nothing else.

- Watch at least three Letterman shows through this clear water.

With the help of a tropical fish store, begin transforming your aquarium into an ecosystem. Do it in stages, watching Letterman throughout every buildup of the aquatic ecosystem.

When it's time to add fish, go to the fish store and make some careful selections. One fish will be named David Letterman. You will also need to get a fish for every member of the band. When you watch the show through this mini-sea, look for the Letterman fish when Dave is talking. When the camera shifts to Paul Shaffer, locate the Paul Shaffer fish.

REGIS PHILBIN

DAVE

LATE NIGHT LETTERFISH II

- Send out invitations to friends requesting their attendance at an "Oceanographic Viewing of the David Letterman Show." Tell them to bring their swimming suits and a snorkel if they have one.

- When they arrive, keep the viewing chamber hidden until it's time for the show to come on. (This may require covering the area with a sheet.)

SULLIVAN'S GHOST

- Allow everyone to slip into their bathing suits and put on their snorkels.

- When everyone is ready, do a countdown of ten to unveil the aquatic viewing arrangement.

- Time this to coincide with the exact beginning of the Letterman Show.

MUJIBUR

LARRY BUD MELMAN

SIRAJUL

ARMADILLO

- Bring out the cameras and video equipment to record this experience of Late Night Letterfish.

- Introduce the fish and allow everyone to have a turn sitting on the best viewing spot.

MADONNA

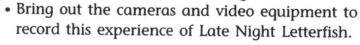
PAUL

NOH AWARENESS

- Purchase a pair of chopsticks and obtain a book of Japanese words. In this book, locate the Japanese words for:

TELEVISION	**JAPAN**	
TRANSFORMATION		**SELF**
OCEAN	**EMPTY**	

- Write each word on a separate piece of paper and fold each piece at least five times.
- For the next month place these folded up Japanese words in front of you whenever you watch the David Letterman Show.
- Throughout the show use the chopsticks to pick up a word, unfold it, and practice recognizing what the word means.

Your job is to learn to recognize these six Japanese words while you watch Letterman. If it takes longer than a month, then continue practicing. You should not rush your learning. The chopsticks insure you will handle the exercise with a sense of caring and respect.

When you can finally recognize all the words, do the following, but only during a show:

- Pull out these two words, "self" and "transformation," and carry them with you for a week looking at them throughout the day. Every once in a while, bring out your words so someone else is able to see them. If someone asks about them, immediately give them to that person as a gift. When they ask what the words mean, say, "You need to learn how to watch the David Letterman Show. Then you will understand these words."

LAUREL CROWNS FOR COMEDY KINGS

- Choose a country you are interested in but have never visited.

- Gather information on this country so you are able to write a letter to its embassy and cite three things you like about its culture.

- In this letter give your best argument as to why their country would benefit from watching the David Letterman Show. You might, for instance, say that you believe the show would be even more appreciated there than it is here. You might also suggest that the best place to begin would be with a foreign exchange program of comedians. This, in turn, could lead to International Centers for the Preservation, Cultivation, and Fertilization of Humor. If there are national poet laureates, then why are there not national **comic laureates**? (While we're at it — why not a Nobel Prize?)

DAVID LETTERMAN ENDOWED CHAIR
FOR LUNACY

- Write a letter to at least a dozen university presidents demanding to know why they don't teach a course on David Letterman.

- Send any response you get to all the other university presidents.

- Say you are considering raising money for a David Letterman Endowed Chair for Lunacy.

JOKE ASYLUM

- Start writing down the jokes you enjoy most on the Letterman Show.

- Select three you believe everyone in the world would benefit from hearing.

- Send these jokes to an embassy and ask if they will keep it in a safe place in case there is a national emergency. Express your hope that their country will have the wisdom to create a depository for the world's diminishing supply of jokes and nonsense.

MU SICK MU SICK MU SICK

- Acquire some tapes or CDs of world music. (They could be of African drumming, Scottish bag pipes, South American flutes, or anything from anywhere.)

- When Letterman talks to a guest, turn on this music from another country's culture.

- Note how the experience of the show changes.

- Experiment with different kinds of music. Report this investigation to someone you believe does not like the Letterman Show.

LETTER TO THE PRESIDENT

- Send a letter to the President or leader of another country asking them to request that David Letterman be given an international post that keeps a watch on humor throughout the world. This person's office would be responsible for noticing when a country's humor is hitting a crisis level. Secret squadrons of comics could then be airlifted to countries in need of laughter.

- Keep sending out letters to foreign leaders until you get a reply.

- When you receive a response, send a copy to every leader who hasn't responded and say that you want to give them another chance to take responsibility for their country's state of hilarity.

- Cite the enclosed letter as an indication that some countries take you seriously.

ADOPT A FOREIGN COUNTRY

- Select a country of your choice.

- Purchase that country's flag, learn one word a week from their language, eat a typical traditional meal, and, most importantly, learn one joke from that country.

Figure out what you must do to learn a joke from another country. Do you contact a foreign restaurant in your area? Do you contact a language teacher? This is your main mission. During a national holiday of that country, call a Letterman fan and tell them the foreign joke.

NO PORTION OF THIS BOOK'S PROFITS WILL BE DONATED TO ANY POLITICAL ORGANIZATION.

POOR OLD TIRED ICE CUBE

- Remove some ice cubes from your freezer and set them in front of your TV, allowing them to watch the David Letterman Show.

- If the show's humor is so hot that the ice melts, place the water in a plastic vial and seal it so it won't leak.

- Mail this to any person or place in the North Pole.

- In a letter, explain you are sending them some very heroic "retired ice cubes" that melted while watching the David Letterman Show.

- Ask them to pour the "retired ice cubes" onto the Arctic ice so that all the ice up there can pick up the good vibrations from Letterman.

- Send along a copy of this book and a videotape of a few Letterman shows.

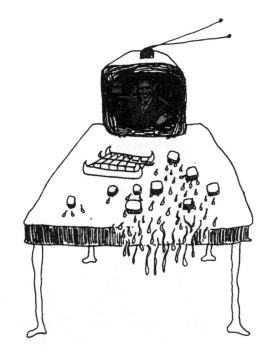

Audience of ice cubes melts before a really hot show.

LETTERMAN CONTRABAND

There are organizations like "Books for Africa" that send books, clothes, and other items to foreign countries.

- Make an appropriate donation to one or more of these organizations, but include copies of your favorite jokes from your collection of David's best.

- Write a note explaining who David Letterman is and that you sent the donated item as a means of smuggling in a little bit of humor.

TWO GONE AND TWO LATE
FOR THE SHOW

One night two people had an argument over whether it was too late for them to watch *Late Show*. One said, "I'm too gone tonight to be present for Dave's show." The other one replied, "That makes two of us."

They went to sleep and each dreamed they had watched The Late Show with David Letterman. Each miraculously saw that the other was going to be a guest on the show.

Unfortunately, they were unable to hear what the other one said because they were awakened by the sound of a flying book that hovered for a few seconds over their TV set and flew out the window. When they went to the window to see this mysterious object, they heard a distant voice chuckling, "You can never be too late or too gone to see the show."

That couple never ever missed another episode of *Late Show*.

DAVE IS DREAMING . . .

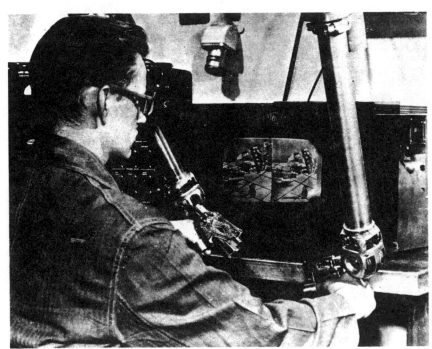

. . . of the TC (technologically correct) way to turn on
a TV.

. . . of a long lost heart throb watching
from the past.

. . . of this advanced viewing exercise which should not be attempted near psychiatrists, parrots, or cattle.

. . . of hyperserious helium heads trying to regain their levity.

Two

Heads Are Crazier

Than One

DAVE'S SECRET RECIPES FOR LOSING WEIGHT

- Drink a glass of your favorite beverage with as many straws as you can.
- Drink the same beverage the next day with one less straw.
- Repeat until you have no straws.

- Arrange your meals so that all of your food is on only half a plate. Keep the other side empty to remind you of what you don't have to eat.
- Continue doing this for each meal until you get accustomed to it. Then stop doing it.

- Stand on a ladder and eat your meals on top of a refrigerator. With each bite say aloud, "I'm really not eating everything beneath my fork."

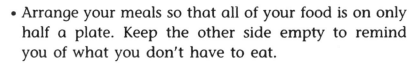

HURRY UP AND TELL YOUR FRIENDS ABOUT THIS BOOK BEFORE BEN AND JERRY RUN OUT OF NEW ICE CREAM FLAVORS.

THE MASTER PIECE

- Purchase the strangest item you can find that costs no more than one dollar.

- Invite at least four other Letterman fans to do this too.

- Gather everyone together with their items.

- All the items in the collection must now be attached to each other using any means available — glue, nails, string — whatever.

When the master piece is done, say to yourself, "This is great, but is it art?" If it is — have a champagne opening! If it isn't, perhaps it's a religious object, so venerate it! Is it a trophy? Award it to the wackiest character in town! A monument? Take it to a park, make a speech, and dedicate it to the spirit of hilarity.

TAKE ME OUT TO THE LETTERGAME

- Place a baseball in your friend's refrigerator.

- Write a note on the ball saying, "If you are reading this ball, please go look under the sink." Make certain that you place a baseball glove under the sink with an envelope attached.

- On the envelope print, "Please Open if You Understand Baseball." When the envelope is opened, the following message will be seen:

Caught You!

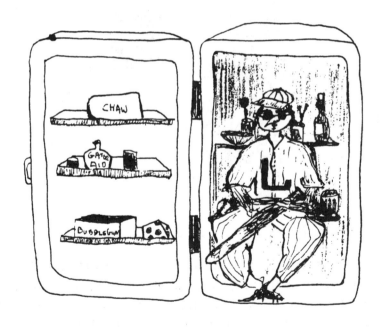

PLEASE APPRECIATE THE FACT THAT DAVE HAS NEVER BEEEN STRUCK OUT BY NOLAN RYAN, SATCHEL PAIGE, OR ALIBI IKE.

"Oh Great Mystery . . ."

ONLY TWO CAN PLAY THIS GAME — I

Do the following exercise with a fellow Letterman fan:

- Practice saying the name "Letterman" in two parts, "Letter" and "man." Let one person say "Letter" and the other say "man." Practice saying this name so it sounds like one person talking.

- When you have rehearsed this enough, go to various stores and purchase small things like chewing gum.

- When you pay, ask the clerk whether he or she watches David Letterman. Take turns asking the question from store to store, but, each time, when you get to that last word, "perform" your duet and see if anyone notices.

- Continue practicing until you are able to do this flawlessly.

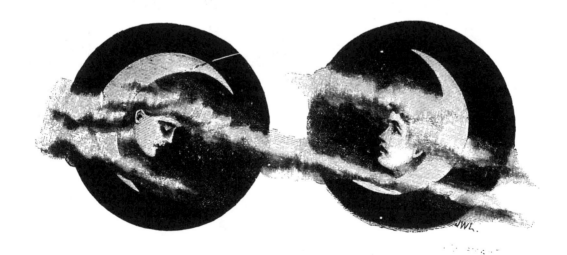

ONLY TWO CAN PLAY THIS GAME — II

- Go to a T-shirt store and have two T-shirts made, one for yourself and one for your significant other or best friend. One shirt should be made with the letters, "LETTE" and the other with the letters, "RMAN."

- Walk around, side by side, wearing these T-shirts.

- Watch people's expressions when they see that the two T-shirts are actually one message.

- Repeat this procedure if you dare, this time making three T-shirts for three of you to wear and walk around in.

- They should say, "LETTE," "R," and "MAN."

*Do you have questions about your health? your finances?
your love-life? religious matters? politics or diet?
Bring all questions great or small to:*

THE LETTERMANTIC ORACLE

- Turn on your radio and tune in to a talk show.

- Turn the volume all the way down and ask your question.

- Immediately turn the radio volume up and listen to what you hear. This is the response to your question.

- Don't like the answer? Turn the volume down and try again.

ANOTHER ORACLE

- Purchase some fortune cookies and place your own fortunes in them.

- Each message should say the following: "Something extremely important to you will be said on the next David Letterman Show."

- The next time you eat at a Chinese restaurant with friends, secretly ask the waiter to replace the after dinner fortune cookies with these "Letterman Fortune Cookies."

AND NOW A WORD FROM OUR SPONSOR:

MEDITATE*: the Letterman Way
LEARN: the Mystic Art of Tube Meditation
STUDY: the Mental Methods by Which DL Leaves the World Behind

BUY
The Lunatic Guide
to the David Letterman Show

*Scientists working with masters of meditation from both terrestial and extra-galactic origins have discerned extraordinary properties in the cathode ray tube (TV screen) when conscious thoughts are directed to its surface. DL has mastered the art of integrating the electrons emitted from the tube with the dynamic forces pouring forth from his eyes.

Hail to the Letter Man

PLUG INTO DAVE

THE LOURDES OF HUMOR

Last Wednesday God communicated with a parrot, teaching the bird to say, "Lourdes of Humor." A tape recording of this holy message was sent to the Pope, who consulted with the ghost of W.C. Fields, now an evangelist for the David Letterman Show in heaven.

Unbeknownst to Fields and the rest, a grasshopper overheard all that was said and revealed in the seance. Using the most advanced insect technology of which he was aware, this dedicated hopper for Dave's show has communicated the entire revelation to us. This is what was *Said* and *Shown* that late night in the Vatican, following a Papal viewing of Letterman:

The next page manifests The Lourdes of Humor, the Pope's Private Gallery of Luna-Saints.

Grasshopper

Vatican Security Agent concealing Pope's TV monitor used for watching Letterman

LUNA-SAINTS

Patron saint of the unstrung

Inventor of Top 10 Lists

The beaming of a Luna-lope

"Secret Luna Message Hidden in Front Teeth Gap"

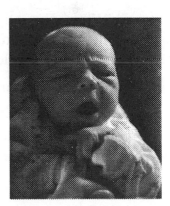

Dave's hairdresser

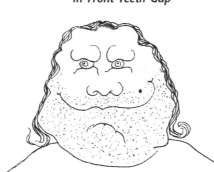

Professor Hilaritas

Luna-Saint of the Little People

DINER DINING DAVID STYLE

- Purchase the tiniest envelopes you can find.

- Place a tiny message into each envelope and attach it, with a paper clip, attach it to a menu at a diner.

- The message should read: "I think David Letterman would order the cheese sandwich."

NOT IT !

- To play the following game of "TV telephone tag," establish a network of local Letterman fans.

- Call another player on the phone at any time during the show.

- When the other player answers, count to five and then check to see if the Letterman audience is laughing. If they are laughing, say, "You're **it**!" If there is no laughter after five seconds, then *you* are "it."

- The game continues as long as Letterman is on, with the person who is "it" calling another player, and so on.

- The person who is "it" when the show goes off the air must purchase a copy of this book and give it to the most serious person they know.

LETTER BUTTER

I received a jar of peanut butter in the mail. The label read: *Letterman Peanut Butter*. When I opened the lid, the room immediately became filled with the distinct identity of peanut aroma. However, when I looked into the jar, I was astonished to find that it was filled not with peanut butter but with tiny little letters.

With a knife, I spread some letters and right in front of my eyes these words took form:

The "pea-" is a friend of our potato dreamer and has asked me to help make you a "nut." When you get too damn serious about things, spread some of these letters on a piece of paper and the silliness you read there will give you the kick in the butt you need to get on with having a ridiculous life.

Letter butter storage unit.

HOW MANY ARE TRUE NUTS?
Many fruits called nuts are not really nuts at all. Of the above, the true nuts are the walnut (a); acorn (b); chestnut (d); pecan (f); filbert (h); and brazil-nut (i). The others are peanut (c); coconut (e); and almond (g), really the kernel of a peach-like fruit.

LOCAL LETTERMAN TOOT-OUT

- Place an advertisement in your local newspaper or post the following announcement on every car windshield in your area:

Let's Toot for Letterman

One week from today, you are invited to participate in a tribute to the importance of humor in our lives. Next Saturday, at twelve o'clock noon, toot your car, truck, or ram's horn for three seconds. The tribute has begun! Everyone must then blow up a balloon (without tying it) and release it, so it zips around in the air. Your mission is to give as many balloons to people as you can and to spread the news of this most honorable event. Tell everyone to let the balloons go at exactly five seconds past noon on Saturday. When the balloon is full of your air and released, shout as loudly as you can:

"Balloons at Noon — Lunacy Soon"

- Recruit a local radio station to give a countdown for the big event.

TELL THEM THAT YOURS IS A LISTENER-SUPPORTED LIFE.

DAVE IN MANY DIMENSIONS

- Make several hundred copies of the following mini-poster:
  Have you ever dreamed that you were watching the Late Show in 3-D?

- Post this poster in public places you think are appropriate or appropriately inappropriate.

Device for sucking Letterman image off the television screen, enabling 3-D encounters.

GIVING DAVE A HAND

- Write this message on the palm of your hand:

Let's give Dave a hand.

- Find three people to show this message to during the day.

- Ask each one whether they watch the David Letterman Show.

- If they say "no," say, "Since you don't watch the show, I can't explain my hand."

- If they say "yes," ask if they saw it three weeks ago on Tuesday.

- If they say "yes," ask if they saw it on Tuesday the week before. See if you can find a night when they did **not** see the show.

- When they admit to missing a show, you may then say that the message on your hand has something to do with the show they missed.

- If they have never missed a show, tell them they don't need to have the message explained. They know already.

THE VIRGIN FINGER

- Pick a finger that is never used to turn on your television set.

- Use that "virgin" finger tonight to turn on the Letterman Show.

- Tomorrow morning, write a small "L" on the tip of that finger and look at it throughout the day.

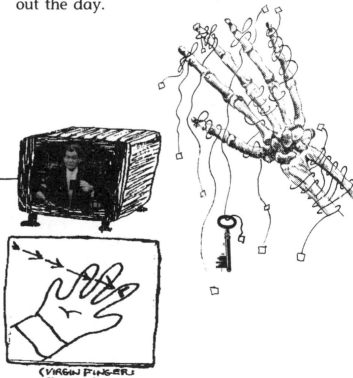

(VIRGIN FINGER DETAIL)

QUALITY CONTROL

- Find someone you know who does not like Late Night.

- Thank them for having volunteered for the important task of disliking the show.

- This will probably confuse them, so explain that a book about the show encouraged you to say this, and that it is necessary for some people not to appreciate Letterman's brand of humor. Without their lack of interest, the show would not be as interesting as it really is.

- Tell this person to keep up the good work and not be tricked by anyone who wants them to like the show.

- Then ask if they would agree to watch Letterman at least once every two weeks in order to maintain their distaste for it.

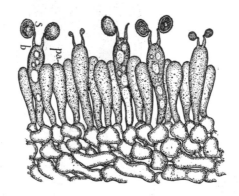

Suflusis aseriosis, *the dust from whose spicules is accredited with inducing wildly fluctuating conditions of spontaneous absurdity*

VIBRATING CHAIR

Uncamouflaged prototype of vibrating chair

- Find someone you believe has a fantastic speaking voice.

- With a portable cassette recorder, tape them reading this announcement:

Tonight David Letterman will attempt to create television history. He will conduct the entire show while sitting in a vibrating chair. The public has not been informed of this historical attempt, though the manufacturer of the vibrating chair has leaked the story. We have an unconfirmed report that this never-before-accomplished feat will take place tonight. Other talk show hosts have tried but failed to get through an entire show while seated on it. Be part of the home audience when Dave makes his attempt. Don't be fooled: the chair is camouflaged as an ordinary chair. Listen for a tremor in his voice. If you hear it, know that broadcast history has been made.

- Play this tape for anyone who needs to be a witness to this event.

WHERE THE GHOST HOST HOVERS

Some people take ghosts very seriously. For instance, have you heard the rumor that David Letterman has *really* seen the ghost of Ed Sullivan? I'm not referring to the silly things Letterman says about Sullivan on his show. I want to know whether anyone has heard that Letterman has actually seen the ghost. After all, there are even things written in books about ghosts, including the ghost of Ed Sullivan, who so vexes David Letterman!

I really hope that Dave is reading this book. Just in case he is, I have placed a special message for his eyes only. If you don't happen to be Dave Letterman, you will find a copy of a portion of this message printed on page 121.

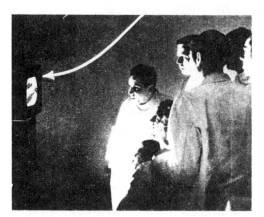

Scientists study Ed Sullivan's ghost and its unbelievable ability to transform into an arrow.

Capturing one point of enlightenment during a Letterman broadcast.

Dear Dave,

I want you to know that there is a way to take care of the ghost of Ed Sullivan. The procedure has been blessed by a tiny African village in Zimbabwe. Mark a spot on your stage floor and place a sign near it, saying, "Do not stand on this spot. It is reserved for Mr. Sullivan." Your entire staff is to be informed that no one, under any circumstance, is to stand on that spot. It is to be protected from the presence of any human form. That spot is strictly for ghosts. It cannot be haunted by human beings.

In a seance conducted by a very large medium, we contacted Ed Sullivan's agent. He told us that Ed never missed standing on the spot he was told to stand on during a live show. His opinion was that Ed's ghost is looking for that spot. Once he has found it, he will remain there forever. He advised us to find a spot for Mr. Sullivan.

It's that simple. Where else would you find Mr. Sullivan than in the building having his name printed on it? He's definitely not lost. It's up to you to find a spot where the ghost host can go on with the show.

The Author

DAVE IS DREAMING OF THE LUNACY LABORATORY

Embassy of Lunacy

Lab technician searching for lunacy

The inventor of David Letterman

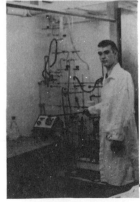

The author during his internship at the Lunacy lab

Janitorial broom in use at the embassy **(facing page)**

The
Hidden Meanings

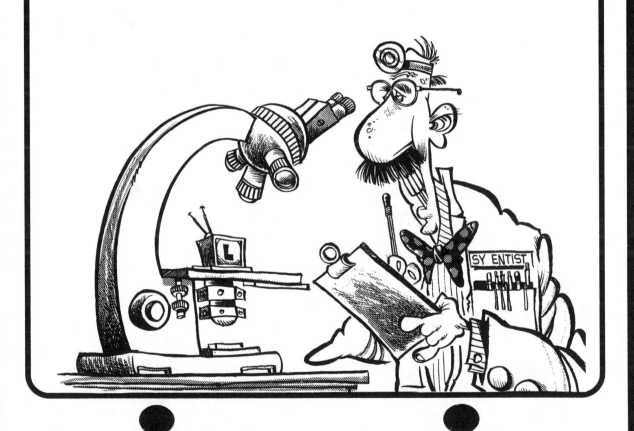

of

The
David Letterman
Show

BIG AND SMALL

- Stare at these two images:

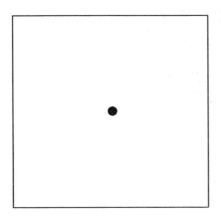 

- Imagine that you could shrink to the size of a tiny insect so that the dot on the left would seem to be as big as the image of Dave on the right.

- Now imagine yourself as big as a whale so that the image of Dave is as small as the dot.

- Now imagine you are a dot as big as a whale or a whale as small as a dot or a Letterman face on the body of a whale or a dot the size of a whale on the forehead of a Letterman as big as a . . .

- Get it?

THIS BOOK IS NEITHER A RADISH OR A TURNIP.

SENDING OUT AN S.O.S.

- You are stranded on a desert island with a TV that only picks up *Late Show*. (You have decided that you don't want to be rescued because you have come to an amazing understanding of life as a result of watching Dave. You are completely at peace with your situation on the island.)

- Wanting to share this understanding with the world, you decide to send a **message in a bottle.**

- With this in mind, compose a short note and put it in a real bottle.

- Take this bottle to your local library and leave it on the shelf where self-help psychology books are kept.

- In the weeks to come, try to imagine all the ways your message might add a little lunacy to the lives of the good people who frequent the library.

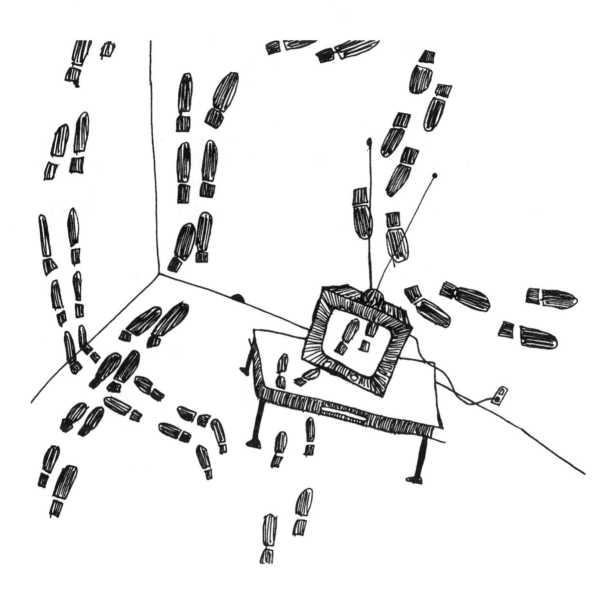

WALKABOUT

- Take a life-size photograph of the bottom of your left shoe.

- Take a life-size photograph of the bottom of your right shoe.

- Go to a copy shop and make one hundred copies of each photograph.

- Pin or tape these copies to the walls of the room where you watch the *Late Show*, so that it looks like an invisible person wearing your shoes were walking up and down the walls!

- Continue putting up these footprints so that they travel all the way around your room —up one wall, across the ceiling, down the other wall, across the floor, all over the furniture, round and round again.

- When you finish walking about your TV viewing environment, sit in the middle of the floor and contemplate these footprints.

- Now let your mind *walk* wild!

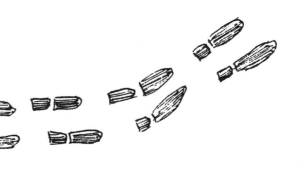

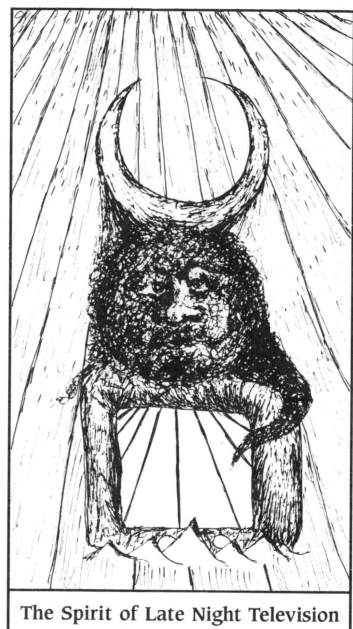

The Spirit of Late Night Television

HIDDEN MEANINGS
IN THE DAVID LETTERMAN SHOW

- Consider the meaning of the word "meaning." Pull this word apart and find what the word is hiding. You will see that it hides the word, "mean." In what sense is a meaning mean? Is it mean because it keeps its meanness hidden? Or is its meanness a clue to the meaning of meaning?

- With these questions in mind, watch a Letterman show and keep tabs on how many times a guest is nice to Dave and how many times he or she is mean.

- At the end of the show, add up the score. If he or she wasn't mean, then say to yourself, "This show had no meaning." If he or she was mean, then say to yourself, "The mean-ing of the show is three." If he or she has a larger nice score, say, "It is difficult to find the mean-ing in this show. It has too much competition."

- Do this every night for a week. During the day, practice developing a new understanding of mean-ing. Give mean-ing less importance in your life.

Bonus meaning:

- Pull apart the word, "meaning" in this way: "Me, an ing." Now you will find another hidden meaning more deeply hidden than the previous one we uncovered. This meaning is a statement about your self-identity. It is a confessional statement where you admit to being an "ing." It may surprise you to know that an "ing" is another word for meadow or pasture. With this understanding, your search for meaning may have something to do with an unconscious fantasy of being a meadow. Perhaps you are the reincarnation of a meadow or pasture.

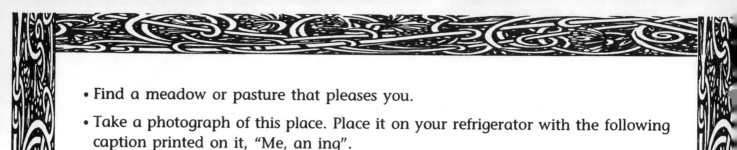

- Find a meadow or pasture that pleases you.

- Take a photograph of this place. Place it on your refrigerator with the following caption printed on it, "Me, an ing".

THE GOLDEN EAR

Once upon a time a farmer in Indiana grew a field of corn. On a particularly hot day in August, the farmer found something incredible in his field. While taking an afternoon stroll, he came across an unusual gold piece of corn. On a stalk was a perfectly shaped piece of corn made of pure gold. At first he thought someone was playing a trick on him, but he knew there was no way the gold could have been that carefully wrapped inside the corn husk.

He took the whole corn plant to his house and showed all the neighbors. Soon people began to point out that a gold piece of corn must be worth a lot of money. The farmer began wondering whether it was worth enough to help him solve his mortgage problem with the local bank. He had been very worried about his family's financial situation and had prayed long and hard for some help. Maybe, he thought, his life had become like one of those fairy tales his grandmother used to read to him when he was a young boy.

It didn't take long for him to pull the gold piece of corn out of its stalk and take it to a gold trader. The gold trader said he could only give him what the gold was worth on the basis of how much it weighed. I have failed to mention that this was no ordinary piece of corn. It was three feet in length and required a team of mules to carry it. The corn, to the farmer's great delight, was worth a lot of money. He had enough to clear his mortgage and take a long-awaited trip to visit his sister.

The farmer then remembered something. This was not just a large piece of corn

A BEAUTIFUL SPECIMEN OF FISHERMAN'S LUCK

that happened to be made of gold. What he had found was a biological miracle. This corn had actually grown on his field and was not made by man. He persuasively told the gold trader that its value must be greater than its weight in gold. It was a genuine corn miracle.

The gold trader said, "I'm sorry. That's the best I can do." An old friend of the farmer who took care of his mules replied, "Yep. You've got yourself into a real pickle. Since you pulled that corn off the stalk, no one will ever believe it grew out of the ground. All you have now is a block of gold." The farmer was saddened by the realization that no one would be able to appreciate the miracle of the corn and understand its true meaning. Since he had pulled the corn off its stalk, its meaning would be lost to everyone else. The farmer went ahead and sold the golden corn. He paid off his debts and spent the rest of his life thinking about how he had found a great miracle and had let it slip out of his hands. The true meaning of the corn could not be shared or realized by anyone else. Many years after the farmer died, a young boy from Indiana was playing in the former farmer's field. He, too, came across a stalk of corn. In this stalk was another miracle, just as miraculous as the one made of gold. In this stalk was a parchment made of corn powder. On this parchment was written the story you are now reading. This boy grew up to be a man who knew that hidden meanings are only valuable if they are hidden. He became a famous host and comedian. He eventually moved to New York City and found more gold than he knew what to do with.

MR. TIFFANY'S SECRET

It is a well-known fact that Mr. Tiffany understood the magic of glass more than anyone who has ever lived. His staff created incredible works of art that are still revered by collectors and visitors to the world's greatest museums. Unfortunately, he kept his techniques and formulas secret and nothing was ever written down. The achievements of Tiffany will never be duplicated again. The magic in glass he successfully harnessed is lost forever.

But then again, maybe not. In the early days of radio, before there was such a thing as television, Tiffany's grandson appeared on the scene. No one knew who his grandfather was and he lived by himself in an apartment over Carnegie Hall. He became well known as the greatest sound effects master of all time. The top radio networks used him to get the right feeling for their dramatic productions. He was in great demand and made a small fortune.

There was one thing about him that was most unusual. In his contracts, he always specified that he must be able to choose one sound in any production he works with. Everyone took this as the quirky nature of an eccentric. After all, the effects those sound people designed were often made from strange recipes. For instance, the sound of mild rain would be produced by rubbing a mike stand with excelsior, whereas a torrential downpour was obtained by pouring salt on waxed paper or crisp lettuce, or rattling peas in a sieve.

Tiffany's grandson was best known for two things. The first was his reputation for making the best thunder in the business. He would mount a copper window screen to a frame and connect an eight-inch spiral wire that acted as a phonograph needle in transmitting the screen's vibrations to an electrical pickup sent to an amplifier. When the screen was hit by a soft-headed drumstick it made the best summer thunder you ever heard. Sometimes people got out their umbrellas when they saw him carrying that screen. It was that real.

But the thunder wasn't what he was most known for. It was that quirk I previously mentioned about his having to choose one of his own sound effects for every radio

drama he ever worked on. People thought it peculiar that he chose the same sound in every play. Wherever he worked, he chose to introduce, in at least one moment of the play, the sound of breaking glass. It came to be that everyone who knew him or knew of him called him "the glass man." He made the best sound of breaking glass that anyone ever heard.

When the old radio days were finished, the glass man retired. He went to live in the woods of Canada. Years later, a young comedy writer was hiking in these woods and he came across the man, who by now was quite old and even more eccentric than he had been in his youth. The old man put forth his hand and said, "You can call me Glass Man." The young comedian introduced himself and asked why the man was called "Glass Man." They sat down on an old log and the comedian heard the same story I have already told you. After the story, the Glass Man told him something else and I only know a little of it.

The Glass Man told him he was actually the grandson of the original Mr. Tiffany. Furthermore, he confessed that his grandfather had told him the secret of harnessing the magic of glass. He didn't want to follow his grandfather's footsteps and didn't want anyone to know who he was. He enjoyed his privacy too much for that. He chose a career having nothing to do with light. He chose a career in sound. What is important to realize is that the secret of harnessing the magic of glass was the same secret he used to become a famous sound man.

I do not know what the secret was, but I have found a few clues. The secret of harnessing the magic of glass has to do with spontaneously breaking glass. The breaking must be spontaneous. It must be associated with the sound of laughter, and it must be a window that holds the glass. That's all I know. The old glass man gave the Tiffany secret away that day and made the young man promise he would not try to make lamps. He told him he was free to pursue any other career except the production of stained glass.

This man eventually became associated with the David Letterman Show. I'm not sure who he is. He might even be David Letterman himself. But of this I am sure. You now know one of the hidden secrets of the David Letterman Show. There is no way you will be able to hear the sound of that breaking glass in the same way.

A Leprechaun Story

A long time ago in the green emerald called Ireland, lived a leprechaun. This leprechaun loved music. He loved it so much he couldn't stop singing and hearing music. He begged his parents for a piano, but, unfortunately, leprechauns don't have pianos. They only play the flute and drum. But this leprechaun was a clever one. He kept teasing his parents with his silly lyrics until they finally said, "We're getting too old to laugh so hard. You're going to have to stop singing so many of those silly songs. We can't take it."

"The only way I can stop," the young leprechaun replied, "is if I have a keyboard to keep my musical mind occupied." The parents at this time were ready to do anything. They were insanely desperate. They granted his wish and took him to a great stone in the forest.

At the base of this stone, he was told to say his name and sing a song, a great song that could be heard by every living creature in the forest. His parents then said with timid hesitation, "We should tell you this. We don't know what will happen if you ask for some keyboards. We've always been told to not ask for them. No one, as far as we know, has ever asked. We've never met or heard of a leprechaun with a keyboard."

That warning didn't curb the youngster's desire to play his music. He sang his song and shouted then and there that he wanted, more than anything else, to be completely surrounded by keyboards.

The earth began to shake as if the whole forest were the surface of a monstrous drum being played by a drum stick the size of the largest tree on the land. A green cloud descended upon the family and, for five minutes, I'm told, the most beautiful piano music was heard throughout all of Ireland. When the music stopped, the cloud lifted and the boy was nowhere to be seen.

Rumor has it, among every leprechaun I've ever talked with, that the boy turned into a hybrid creature, part leprechaun and part human. Among human beings, such a creature is called a "musician." This musician awoke to find himself in the midst of an ocean of keyboards and can be seen every night on the David Letterman Show.

THE LITTLE PEOPLE

The little people, as they are sometimes called by those who have seen them, live under the earth just outside New York City. These people are not people in the sense that we understand one another. I must admit I'm not exactly sure who they are or where they originally came from. Maybe they're leprechauns or maybe they are aliens from another planet. I do know that many people, particularly entertainers and authors of books, have seen them.

I met someone who once was able to spend a weekend underground with a group of them. I won't yet reveal his name, but I checked him out and, sure enough, the little people told me they had visited with him. During the weekend, he discovered what some of us already know. The little people can only communicate through

lists. If you ask one of them a question, the little person will respond with a list of ten answers. The lists are never, ever serious. They are always absurd and filled with absolute lunacy. It takes some getting used to when you first hear them talk to one another. They are able to think and say these lists with incredible speed.

During that weekend, the little people told him they had decided to invade the surface world. It was time for the human race to be introduced to their wisdom. Humans had suffered long enough in ignorance and the little people felt sorry for them. They could no longer selfishly withhold their wisdom and knowledge.

The little people chose the David Letterman Show to be the central distributor of their wisdom. To protect themselves, they sent out a rumor that David Letterman was actually an alien from another planet. This would keep the humans looking up at the sky rather than looking underground. This was done as a safety precaution.

The delivery of their wisdom is given in the form of lists. That is the only way they know how to communicate. They beam up a list before every show. It is received in the minds of a group of comedy writers who believe it is their own creativity generating the list. In this way, the little people are secretly teaching human beings their wisdom.

I now want to tell you the most important part of the story. The man who spent a weekend with the little people is a relative of mine. I know his story to be true, not only because of what the little people said, but because of his reputation as a scholar and a gentleman. On the last night of his visit, he stayed awake so he could sneak into the little people's library. It was an enormous structure with very complicated stairwells and contained thousands of television monitors, videocameras, Tiffany lamps, sculptings of vegetables cast in solid gold, and bizarre sound effect devices. When he opened the door to the main reading room, he found that, although there were thousands of books, every book was the same book. When he opened the one book, it had only one paragraph. This is what he read:

> *You, my dear reader, only need to understand one thing. The gold that everyone wants to find has been given many names. Humans keep making the same mistake over and over again. They mistake the name of gold for the gold itself. The gold cannot be seen through any lens. The glass must be broken so you may see. Furthermore, the gold can't be heard by any ear. It sometimes takes an entire field of ears to help one human hear.*

> *The gold you desire is only fully recognized in the music that speaks directly to your soul. Humans try to explain the creation of music and all the other arts as due to fictional attributes or mechanisms like "creativity." There is nothing human that creates. It is the whole world, the entire field, that creates. The door to entering this field or pasture of play is closed by seriousness but re-opened by lunacy.*

> *The fullest transformation of one's self is in the becoming of an "ing." When the meanness of meaning is turned into its opposite, the truth of an open field with nothing but space is brought forth. In this vast empty space, one beholds the gold. At that time, one may begin transforming self into the gold alchemists have always known and purposefully forgotten. There is no other understanding. This is all you need to stand under you.*

Upon reading that paragraph the young man experienced enlightenment. The whole of eternity was shown to him. He ran with the book to a mirror and noticed that his body was the same, but his self was gone. The person who visited the little people was a very close relative of mine. It was the self I used to be.

As I stood in front of the mirror and said outloud, "Me, an ing," I heard the laughter of hundreds of the little people. They knew I had become one of them.

A great party and feast was held the next day. It was filled with more laughter than any "self" would be able to handle. Completely intoxicated with the birth of this magical mirth, I fell asleep. When I awakened, I was back in my old home. I looked at the clock and knew it was time to get to the typewriter and do some work. As I stumbled toward my desk, a tiny note fell out of my pocket. I picked it up and read:

DON'T FORGET TO WATCH LETTERMAN.
HE'S ONE OF US.

Your companions in lunacy,
the little people

CROSSING OVER

- Place your personal copy of *The Lunatic Guide to the David Letterman Show* on top of a table.

- Sit down so that you face the book.

- Open it to any page and read the first three words.

- Place the book down and turn it around so that it now appears upside down.

- Get up from your chair and walk to the other side of the table so that you are able to read the book again.

- Say outloud, "Dave, thanks for helping me cross over to the other side."

"That's all folks." (for now)

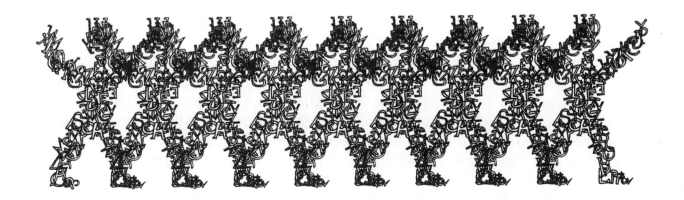

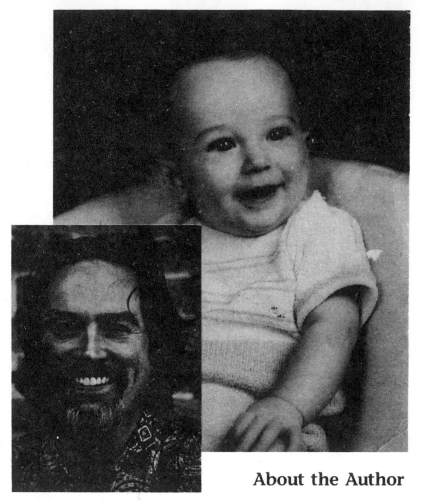

About the Author

Bradford Keeney, Ph.D., is Professor at the University of St. Thomas, St. Paul, Minnesota, and author of numerous books including *Shaking Out the Spirits: A Psychotherapist's Entry into the Healing Mysteries of Global Shamanism* and the forthcoming *The Lunatic Guide to The Grateful Dead: Crazy Wisdom Tales for Dead Head Enlightenment*. Internationally renowned for his contributions to psychotherapy, he presently lectures on therapeutic ways of watching *The Late Show With David Letterman*. He is an improvisational pianist, composer, an evangelist for lunacy, absurdity, and the ridiculous, and a member of The Omsemble Orchestra with Charles Stein and George Quasha.